SPEAKING WITH A BROKEN MIRROR
by John Rolens

Fragments

Fragments of a broken mirror;
When did it fall?
Each piece reflects a part.
Each piece reflects it all.

A Kaleidoscope of memory
changing at the slightest twist.
Colors etched onto an aging thought
where songs of yesterday persist.

Waiting for my turning hand,
random pattern unexpected
seeking out the symmetry
where beauty was perfected.

Eloquent Books
New York, New York

Eloquent Books
An imprint of AEG Publishing Group
845 Third Avenue, 6th Floor - 6016
New York, NY 10022
www.eloquentbooks.com

ISBN 978-1-60693-906-2 1-60693-906-8

Printed in the United States of America

Book Design: Linda W. Rigsbee

Back cover photograph of the author by Josh Rolens

Table of contents

4

MISTY

Poems from E-Mail to Diane

Soft Good Nights

So anyway, that's
the way it starts,
slowly and with
carefully hidden attention,
almost like tiptoeing
past the nursery door,
not wishing to startle
to wakefulness
this tiny life with
soft and shallow breath.

So, let's meet for dinner.
Dimly lit and tablecloth,
exotic food brought by
foreign waiters.
Their heavy accents
add to the mystery
of who we are,
both strangers to ourselves
and to a younger life.
Both ask in silence,
"Do I take the risk?"
Mellow conversation—
Is this how?
Is this what I say?—
spiced lightly with
a little tension, maybe
not too sweet desert,
a little laughter.

May I call you?
Yes.
Soft good nights.

So, shall we see a movie
and dinner first?
Silence weighs heavy
the hesitation of response.
Perhaps too much?
Perhaps, but no.
Dinner and a movie then,
soft good nights.

So, anyway,
we share a plate of pasta.
We share a salad.
We share easy conversation.
We share a movie.
(Somewhere there is a pain we shared.
Dare we take the risk?)
Want to hold her hand
but don't.

Her kitchen bright and friendly
fragrance of the tea
touching both of us
across the table.
It's getting late.
Her lips brush mine.

Soft good nights.

Sleep Well

It is the best time of the day
after colors spill across
the sky like wine dropped
and splashed upon
white linen of a tablecloth
and fireflies echo memories
of the sunshine
of the day just past,
its troubles and concerns
lost within the serenade of
nocturnal creatures,
small, unseen.

Up above, in the darkness
studded with the tiny silver
fires of far-off worlds,
I search the universe until
my spirit brushes soft
across your cheek
and I feel your heart beat
within my chest.
It is then I say
"Good night, Diane.
Sleep well."
This is the best part
of the day.

Feeling the Lawn

I love to cut my grass.
O course there is the aroma,
an occasional sneeze,
but I feel like I have made something
fresh and neat for just a little while
and for just that little while
I get to enjoy that feeling.
After a few days the lawn starts
looking a little ragged again,
or I worry because there has been no rain.
The grass turns brown and cannot grow.
As much as I like having cut my grass,
I wonder why I never say,
"Oh, goodie, wow! I get to cut my grass!"
A job?
A negative view of responsibility?
God, the all-knowing,
God, the master planner of the universe
is responsible for me. After all, he made me,
I am his child.
I want to feel what He feels when He catches
me with wrinkles across my forehead or
a drop of sadness in the corner of my eye.
I want to feel what God feels when He needs to make
an extraordinary sunset or a bird song or a butterfly breeze
for John, simply because John has a need for it.
I do not want to know what God knows.
I don't want to know His plan.

I want to feel just a little of what He feels
when He is taking care of one of us,
when we look neat and fresh,
when He is cutting the grass.

I want you to feel just a little of what God feels
when He sees you reach out to your children.

Leftovers

It strikes me about leftovers,
meals full of unplanned flavors.
A plate of hot and cold heaps
brings memories of when each was fresh,
and their companion conversations
now no more than drifting aromas,
but still enticing if
there is an appetite
for the echoes of past suppers.

The refrigerator is all but empty now,
but clean and ordered and dark—
and cold inside—
until the door is opened
for another meal.

It strikes me about leftovers:
What to do with this kimchi?

Lingering Purple

When it is May and Wednesday slides
across the week with mist, and
shadows go wherever shadows go
to hide from clouds, and the mockingbird
ceases morning greetings,
distant barking dogs and muffled
highway sounds
seem to be in mourning
for the far-off unseen flames
of unreal rapture.
The faithful spiderwort offers purple praises
to the coolness of the day
and waits,
her body to be absorbed
by that holy sun.

Minderings

Sleep came fast last night
and it stayed—
until the alarm beeped.
I don't recall the first electronic
call to routine responsibility.
I awoke instead to the gurgle sounds
of the coffeepot.
A nicer sound anyway,
it lets me fall back into
soft sleep,
full of fuzzy thoughts of
no memorable urgency.
The minderings are more like a primer
for the backyard pump—
to get the cool, clear face splashings going.
Did you ever wash your face by the handsfull,
from an enamel pan that is sitting on
a weathered wooden stand by the side of a well,
the horizon pink giving way to silver blue warmth,
the air chilled,
the water even colder.
The rinsing from a soapless bucket is the best part;
you can swallow handsfull of water
and feel the cold rushing down your throat.
You take in the internal darkness of the earth,
then open your eyes to the brightness of the morning
blurred by silver droplets.

Misty

God, I love this misty weather.
It makes the wipers squeak,
then when you walk in it the feeling is different—
like a walk in the rain but without the rain—
like being almost in love.
Back when we sat across from each other
at India House,
you were maybe a little scared,
but hid it.
I sat there in a fine mist,
almost in love.
Strange, how that has become a precious fragment
of loving you.
There are a lot of little things,
like decaying leaves
wet with mist
scattered on the ground of Eden.
They are the colors we rose up from.
They are the carpet we walk on, touching hands.
They are the bed we lie on.
They are all gifts to the other.

Morning Broke Easy

Morning broke easy over the darkness of October rain.
Rain fell quietly and unannounced
as though not wishing to disturb
my sleep.
(beep-beep and pause and beep)
Unaware, I fell to my routine:
necessity and enjoyment
(symbiotic partners that give meaning to clocks)
I smell the coffee brewing
(sing praises to the inventor of timers)
fix lunch
shave and shower
pay bills, beside a cup of coffee.
(B. B. King makes chores easy)
Still, unrevealed the rain fell quietly,
then kissed me gently on the forehead
as I left the house.
When the day declares itself your lover
and you yield totally to the day's desires,
when that passion has been spent,
you lie in comfort and in peace
between the sheets of dawn and dusk.

My Itch

I guess it is a good thing,
my itch.
At least it is an attention-getter.
Just below the heel of my hand
in the center of my wrist
is the evidence,
the reminder that two days ago,
the late afternoon sun warmed
my bare arms as I tended
to organize the beauty of vegetation
to suit my whim.

I must remember not to be so arrogant
as to call ivy a weed, much less a poison one.
It would be better to see its individual beauty,
to recognize a face in a crowd.
What is that, other than respect?
After all, it is only a weed if I say it is.
It is only poison if I show it no courtesy.
So, I'll let my eyes rest gently on the ivy,
spread forgiving, soothing salve
upon my blemishes.

Sometimes I look for lessons.
Sometimes they are just there
if I pay attention.

Raking Up Thoughts

I keep thinking I should step out onto the patio.
The smoking people seem happy to be out there.
I think they may be enjoying the weather as much
as their cigarettes, or maybe it's the company.

I look at them and remember this morning,
taking in the flowerbeds and
the comfort of the air,
the splashes of sun on my bare arms.
Wouldn't it be great if you could rake up those
little instances from here and there—
like colored leaves
into a huge pile, and then divie into them,
like our black lab, Max, beside himself with joy,
all legs and tongue and tail.

Or, lie on your back in that same pile,
look up at the beauty that is yet to fall,
patches of blue, blue sky and remnants of sun
teasing your eyes,
coaxing the tears to slide down your dusty cheek
until you have to close your eyes against the brilliance,
and you drift away on the fragrance of autumn,
the fragrance of a life well lived,
and you know—you have always known—
the only thing you need to know.

Serious Conversation

A wet morning with its gray skies,
a memory of passion settling
on soft pillows and
tossed sheets,
I wait for the clock to
beep-beep-beep
and end the comfort of this half-sleep.
Then it is only I, bumping through
otherwise empty rooms listening
for the echoes of our moaning
and shouts of yes,
finding peace only in
trailing conversations of
things held in our hearts,
we alone
together.
I walked you to your car and said,
"Goodnight."

THE AGGRAVATION OF

A HUNDRED MES

Power Outage, December 2006

Benedictine and brandy brings a sweet glow
to last night's ice storm.
The afternoon sun glinted through the glass forest.
Sparkling branches popped like burning hardwood
and last summer's snap peas—
memories echoed through a different season.
Fallen branches, fallen lines darken Christmas lights
and chill the empty rooms where window-ice flowers spread,
opaque from lingering breath of last night's children.

Beauty of the golden brandy through a crystal snifter,
reflecting golden flames that cast vague shadows
on the walls like clumsy, brittle questions behind a hallowed eye.
A question trickling from a thawing heart, encased in crystal grief,
erodes, cuts deeper and leaves the lines of age, like rivers
flowing through the barren sands of killing lands.
The flame-cast silhouettes of toy soldiers hang from pine boughs
that will wither rootless in January's chill, and pronounce
in brown and brittle voice, their passing, devoid of any value.

Brandy, sweet to tongue, burning trickle, golden in the eye
child of beauty warmed by hearth and hand,
and born of monks who live cloistered behind their cold, gray stone,
release your aromatic question:
When did a child not die in vain?
So build this abbey, stone on heavy stone until there are no more
and we have given worth to dead ideals
that echo through these cold and sunless halls

like muttered hymns forgotten by the living.
Or honor last night's child born golden, flowing through our veins.
Questions are for those who live; death requires no answers.

New Genesis

She died on March 23, 2003.

Fridays are all anticipation.
All week you know they are coming.
You design them in your mind,
in that deep little pool in your mind
where memory and imagination are
the light and dark of the new genesis.
After a routine Thursday night
the sun rises on reality, or
the clouds attempt to conceal the reality of "No, this is how it is."
Then it comes,
the realization that all week you were
living that which you were designing Friday to be.
All the joys and sorrows of that day
have been spent.
All of the emotions that were to wave
from some golden standard, in
celebration of your creation,
hang motionless in the relaxed brightness
of continuing life,
in the calmness of Friday, March 23, 2007.

Personal Relationships

The weather has been absolutely beautiful here
the last few days.
It has brought with it the
sights and smells and sounds that give you that
ah-new-new-life-falling-in-love kind of feeling.
Falling in love is, more than anything else,
a total acceptance of anticipation while wearing
rose-colored glasses.
Nothing can go wrong.
Anyway, in spring the fancy turns to love.

Besides loving spring,
I have a personal relationship with her.
She fills my heart with
smiles and tears.
I accept that she has her fearful storms—they pass.
Spring and I have defined our relationship.
Yes, I love her, a burden
that is unconditional.
Our relationship, however, has conditions.
When she begins her windy rant,
I retire to the root cellar and converse
with last summer's produce,
which, by the way, is from
the seeds of springs past.

Tell me about your spring,
like you told me about your Halloween,
like you told me about you and the sea.
Tell me about your spring,
with and without the rose-colored glasses.

Icy-Hot

Daylight saving time came early this spring;
Five o'clock came early this morning.
The snooze button kept interrupting Bartok.
I bumbled through a chilly, empty house,
carrying with me the fading fragrance of
last night's Icy-Hot and memories of your delicate fingers rubbing
the small of my back.
Old men with young lovers.

There is a lot to be said for a house inhabited by one person,
but I guess the best thing is
the total and unrestricted use of two bathrooms,
a fact that brings with it the realization that
bathroom doors are an ostentatious display of modesty ...
were it not for Diane's frequent company.
In fact the only reason there is for me to shut the bathroom doors
is to view the artwork they hide if left open.

Bathrooms make good galleries.
You can lie naked in warm water and contemplate art.
Then, in the mirror,
you can see life backwards and
pretend that those are water wrinkles.
Old men with young lovers.

Spring Day, Third Grade, 1949

There is a smell of spring rain
evaporating from the asphalt edges of puddles
scattered about the playground.
There is laughter following the foot stomp
of big kids splashing small kids.
There is the strange feeling of too much heat
for an April day.
There is the sound of a bell announcing
the end of lunch.

When lunch is over
and banana peelings have been stuffed
into brown paper bags, and those stuffed into trash cans,
and the last apple core has gone skittering across
the schoolyard,
the smell of chalkboard chalk permeates the air.
The windows open and the breezes
wrap themselves around the lesson whispers
of that mean old Miss Beshenstein,
then the only thing that has any meaning is three o'clock
or, if the breeze is just right,
the sweat smell from
Angela's hair.

Stop to Pull the Weeds

The smell of last night's rain
the hint of garbage fragrance
I pull the trash can up the white stone drive,
contents already ravaged by raccoons.
Place it by the road for fortune seekers
and the large steel jaws
of trucks monogrammed with WM.

Walk back toward the house—
spring flowerbed
begging me to pull a weed—I do.
Water spots on fresh shined shoes,
I will not wipe them off
but when I get to work
prop my feet upon my desk
and read my spotted shoes
like tea leaves in the bottom
of a cup.

Looking Out My Window
Watching Spring Snow

April snow white on green
silently chooses where to meet in
soft congregations
attracted only to the living,
leaving uncovered and ignored
the dark, hard things of man.
I am taken back to mid-July
and snowy Yellowstone,
alpha and omega,
touring woods and meadows
that embraced the falling snow,
touring lifeless pools
that consumed without consideration
the falling, crystal reverence.

The ravenous passions of
dark, deep Earth devoured the seeds
of life, held back her diamonds,
held back her jade.

It was a vast area of emptiness
with wisps and columns of steam
rising, drifting from here and there.
Primeval, primordial broth,
Earth's water had broken.
The smell of sulfur is not
the smell of Satan's breath.
It is the fragrance of
one flowering chromosome.

Waited,
I stood and waited,
stood and watched for something,
an insignificant tiny motion maybe,
something I could call ancestor
to come swimming toward me,
grow legs and come crawling
from the water.
I had forgotten about time and
my inability to wait for eons.

There is no waiting.
April snow will trickle into May.
The green of spring will push against
this window.
Wisps and columns
of my work,
rising from this barren desktop
will remind me
Eden is never very far away.

A Gentle Assumption

Where is it, the thing I have need of?
Where am I,
the thing I have most need of?
It started last night,
distractions from some parade of thoughts—
the muffled music of the marching band
that long since turned the corner,
following the strutting major—
coffee makers, timers
set to automatic but did not add the water.
It's always a surprise in the morning—
push the lever down,
all that happens
is a little curl of steam
from a heated reservoir,
rinsed and clean.
It's one of those mornings when you think,
"onset."
We all know what onset has come to mean;
tomorrow I will blither,
I will wander off in search of some past thing
that has long since evaporated—
an almost silent curl of steam,
the muffled whisper of last night's rinse water.
An assumption of course.
Maybe Alzheimer's is really
the ultimate level of

passive-aggressive behavior.
Wouldn't that be a bitch?

Morning coffee,
once it brewed, was really enjoyable
in the cool of daybreak.
I just sat passively on the porch,
taking in every thing spring—
creating a place to visit
from behind a blank stare
when what's her name drops by
to deliver a monologue,
occasionally shouting my name,
because I look so very far away—
because I've disappeared around the corner.

Doorman

Another pretty morning at Spanish Pond. It was quiet too. I heard no dogs, which probably means the deer were not out grazing anywhere near. Perhaps they migrate throughout the week. I think I will not try to keep track. To do that feels like it is tied to control. It is like somehow if we know the pattern we are in control, like we have put the thing in a box whose sides are constructed of corrugated explanations. An interesting thought: Is curiosity nothing more than a quest for control? Is serenity and satisfaction the laying aside of desire for control, acceptance of what is. I see a deer in the morning and enjoy her. Tomorrow morning I do not see the deer and I enjoy her not being there. I have no desire to build a corral to keep deer in (or out.) It is good that I get to choose. Somewhere there is a man or women who if they had not been curious and desired control I would be dead from cancer. I hope that someday they can relax with a few of my poems and experience some sort of healing. Healing is a doorway to a whole new world. Have you ever wanted to be a doorman?

Morning Conversations

Sweet cool mornings slip past.

Conversations with sisters, brothers, sons, daughters slide down interstates and disappear into offices, file drawers, e-files placed there by the listeners, talkers, tellers of things important to the past, hearers of tomorrows and tomorrows dissolve like deep concerns and shallow dreams into ordered memories, indexed and waiting for tree frogs, moon glint, street light shadows of Venetian blinds that lay like ladder rungs across the sleepless bedroom walls.

Sweet cool evenings slip past conversations with sisters, brothers, sons, daughters.

Familiar voices carry words, climb the stillness of the night and drift into the nothingness of sleep, waiting there to drop a thousand meanings into the sweet cool morning.

Do Not Disturb

Diane pushed a button and the screen on her telephone lit up, "do not disturb." Outside her window was the thack-thack-thack of construction hammering, hammering, hammering its way toward completion and an after work cold beer gulped from a brown glass bottle which would be only slightly darker than the washboard abs the iron hard pecs and biceps and the muscle fingers that hold a progression of tools and the bottle that will sweat to the rhythm of the salty cooling liquid that trickled down his shirtless body. His hair, the color of the beer he would be drinking when the tools lie silent, was long and matted to his thick, tanned neck and called to her fingers to hold it tightly and taste the brine of hard work that glistened on his throat. She closed her eyes and became the piece of soft white pine that accepted his sixteen-penny nail. She shuddered with each hammered stroke. *How the hell can I have dinner tonight with that half-bald old man?* she thought.

Feather Beds and Iron

I enjoyed my fresh-painted porch furniture this morning. My new doors too. Then there is the dogwood seedling I planted yesterday, looking small but determined. It was good to be in the dim light of dawn, though the sunrise didn't have much to say. Not so the rooster; he was announcing his pride and presence all over Spanish Lake. I stayed outside through my first cup of coffee. Then I went in for a second cup and sat in the gallery and read. There was music in the background as well as train sounds, you know, rumbles and whistles. It is fun to collect sounds for future meditations while feeling the things of imagination left by another poet's words. I wonder if the sounds don't somehow slip into and become a part of my current understanding of the poem I am reading. I lie in the dark on a feather bed in the attic room of Grandpa's house and listen to the train on the other side of the orchard—a long whistle as it approaches the crossing. Sixty years ago and it is where I read a poem this morning. My whole life is an orange spark of hot iron from the noise of wheel-on-rail. It flashes bright in the roar of darkness. Then it's gone.

Effects of Yesterday

I sit in my gallery in the mornings and read, or contemplate the artwork
that does nothing but hang, or watch my front yard do nothing other
than turn brown or green depending on the time of year and yesterday's
weather. This morning while letting my mind wander around the effects
of yesterday I stumbled across memory. Do you remember "Feather Beds
and Iron?" That occurred to me in the same chair while wandering
around the front lawn. What else has occurred to me is that memory is
the annihilator of time, the destroyer of progression, the fence around my
existence. Memory is like a goose in the barnyard randomly pecking the
ground.

Windows

Outside my window there is bright sun.

There is no shadow dance. The trees are very, very still. The day at rest and I'm alone, waiting for a celebration coaxed by breezes, an invitation to a banquet written on a rift of wind from some approaching thunder shower. I close my eyes and dream to step into a field—the quiet smell of fresh-turned soil or feel warm sand beneath my feet and breathe the salty fragrance of the surf—the harvesting of fish or wheat, fermenting of the August grapes. The hunger of my body satisfied by earth while my spirit dines, as if by candle light, on seasoned meditation.

Tell me about today and you. Tell me about the things you see outside your window. Is the world drifting past like a whisper of special meaning? Can you see your name dancing in the shadows of the leaves— the sun resting gently across your imagination and warming it? Do your thoughts ride the softness of white clouds and express your soul to the endless blue of a clear spring sky? Do you feel yourself in all that your eyes bring to your mind to touch? Can you feel that your spirit is not separate from any of it?

Forgive the Misty Blue of Sage in Bloom

The days that cast no shadows wait in silence for the recognition of their frigid contributions. Offer nothing to them. Compliment a star that does not hide behind a dreary shroud of gray. Shun the sadness of deep winter's death where life runs thick and slow through the veins of the barren trees.

It is gray in Saint Louis. It has been gray all week—not unlike the misty blue of sage in bloom. Last Sunday Diane and I planted some Russian sage in her yard that I took out of my yard to make room for dahlias. It was time for change. I also dug out mums and some iris, all for the sake of change, all for the sake of dahlias. I anticipate large colorful blooms. But since I planted them the sky has been gray. It has been rainy. It was gray yesterday when I got to work where I found a building full of deep grieving. I called my oldest daughter and shared tears with her. I called Diane and shared tears with her. It is good to have people who love you. I went home and stopped crying. I looked out the window of the bedroom, the window of the hospice room, the window that once overlooked the bed of Russian sage, and mums and iris. I looked at the gray skies. I looked at the rain. Then I ironed some cloths. Today I will drive home under gray skies. I will fix dinner for Diane and me. I will turn on some Miles Davis and light a candle and I will look into Diane's face across the table, across the fragrance of supper. Tomorrow the sun will shine. Tomorrow the dahlias will become restless and push toward pure, delicious, brilliant beauty. In August I will have forgotten that the dahlias were born beneath gray skies. In August I will look into their faces and I will see my reflection. How else can we enjoy that which is beautiful but to forgive the gray skies, to forgive the thing that brought us here, to forgive the grief?

Scattered Like Straw

When I planted that little bit of grass this past weekend I thought it would be a hassle watering it every morning for a couple of weeks. But, it is really a pleasant thing to be doing at six thirty in the morning. It's cool, birds singing and neighbors from up the road drive by and honk and wave. I wave back although mostly I don't recognize who they are. They go by too fast and the car windows are dark. I guess all that it means is that I am part of someone's life and they acknowledge that to me. I wonder what else I am a part of that I do not recognize. What things go by so quickly—my attention scattered like straw over tiny, freshly sown seeds—that I do not understand my own significance, things that honk and wave and tell me I am as beautiful as that dahlia over by the kitchen door and I don't hear.

Quitting Time

Workers straggle out of the office at quitting time. I wish whistles still blew and everybody ran for the time clocks. Stick the cards in and hear the clack of the stamp. That carried over meanings from the last day of school in the summer when the bell rang and kids ran from the building with report cards in their hands. You never heard a kid say, "The pressure is off for three months." Kids weren't under pressure. I guess they just saw the release as excitement—bullshit—they did not analyze. They just had fun. Sometimes I would work a little late and be the last to leave the International Silver factory up in Wallingford, Connecticut. When the factory is empty and the machines are dead silent the time clock stamp sound echoes around the vast empty area above the machinery, then settles into the oil-soaked wooden floors. Once in eighth grade I stayed late on a half day to help Miss Updike. The bell still rings when the school is empty. When the clapper stops the sound echoes around the halls and comes to rest in shiny, oiled, cork floors or slips over the rail and down the empty space of the three-story stairwell, the deep empty space where Timmy Applegate threatened to jump to his death. Mr. Harget pulled him back over the rail. Images have echoes that are never absorbed. They never find a softness that will accept them, where they can rest. They create their own vast hollow space and never cease their resonance.

Timmy went to School at The Military Academy at Mexico, Missouri—away from home.

The Rhythm of Chaos

I woke this morning at about one thirty. It took me a while to recognize the rhythmic sound that was a wind chime. I do not recall having ever heard a wind chime that kept a constant rhythm. Even after I decided it was a wind chime, I didn't believe it. It had to be mechanical, like the scissor-sharpening man, pushing his cart across my porch; "clang-clang-clang-clang." Finally the wind did something or a night creature buzzing by bumped his head and the sound became random and inconsistent. When half asleep, I prefer chaos to intelligent design. I don't want to think about the scissor man or God or random rhythms. I just want to drift back into sleep. Sleep and chaos hold no complications. Of course, neither did the scissor man. He was straight and to the point.

I Awoke this Morning in Ireland

Sometime last night the rain woke me.

It was coming hard, like a Wagnerian opera. I lay in my safe bed somewhere between half awake and half asleep while the percussion section played images for me and the images sang arias and the arias led me to places of the past that only exist in the nether land bordered by my morning sheets and scrunched up pillows.

Sometime last night the rain came hard.

This morning, outside my back door, there were roses wearing diamonds and a feeling of restoration rode the heavy, damp coolness of the sunless morning, and age left me, but youth did not greet me.

In the stead of all things baptized with human significance there was nothing but the green and wet celebration of my existence.

And what is it in this body that causes it to move?

What is this thing I love?

Zen and the Art of Sleeping

The morning greeted me thirty minutes ahead of the alarm clock. But,
I stayed in bed and let my thoughts run where they would. At first they
flipped through my checkbook looking for something to worry about.
That was a futile effort and my worry snake slithered off into oblivion.
I have no recollection of what followed except for an occasional urge
preceding the conscious reasoning that if I would get up to use the toilet
then maybe I could drift back to sleep. My muscles, however, were totally
disconnected from the powers of logic so I lay there enjoying, in a warped
sort of way, the Zen-like contrast of half-sleep comfort juxtaposed with
bladder stress, wetting the bed not being an option. Richard Strauss
abruptly encouraged me to go piss by blasting the fourth and fifth notes
of *Thus Spake Zarathustra* through my clock. I wanted Zen not Nietzsche,
the difference of night and day, Buddhist and Lutheran.

I think it should be called a startle clock. There is nothing alarming about
it. Maybe a dread clock.

August Morning

Mornings are important in August in St. Louis. One might even honor them by drinking fresh coffee on a shaded patio or on an un-shaded one before the sun comes up. Get up before the sun and turn the impact sprinkler on, you know, the kind that beats a rhythm for a bit and then says shhhhhhhhhhhh while it resets. That sound is a good companion in the dark side of dawn and it compliments the twilight birds who sing the coolness of the day and flutter feathers in the spray. Ah, but then there he is, Master Golden Orb, breaking with a searing grin on the edge of Earth and calling through his yellow teeth to desert winds, commanding them to join him in his havoc to all that's green. Heat without a passion upsets the balance, speaks of argument and anger, so I shall turn the water off and seek companionship of that grey machine whose breath is cold as death but offers comfort throughout the brightness of the day.

Between Sadness

It came easy and was noticeable in the darkness only through the silence
between songs from the CD player. Still, the rain sound was gentle and
caressed the mournful voices of "Urban Bluegrass." Sometimes the sad
things of life are sought out; sometimes we seemingly stumble across
them. This morning they were drawn in music and swirled like a light
rain falling in the dim incandescence of the night light. The shadows of
the falling rain, music shadows of the stories of loss, one small seven
watt lamp—there are no sharp lines in the dawn. Nothing is quite seen.
Nothing is quite heard. Some far off storm has sent a cleansing rain but
it is known only in the silence between sadness.

As It Should Be

The grass in the front yard is tall and green. I noticed it when I put
Kermit out for his morning walk. I was up at four forty-five this morning
so I had plenty of time to read, meditate and wax philosophic, an
ordinary morning but just more time for the ordinary.

Revelation: ordinary is a mask, maybe even a shroud we lay over our
surroundings.

Take time to glance under the mask, lift a corner of the shroud and
identify the body: "It is hard to recognize, but yes officer, that's my life."

But I digress: I climbed the stairs this morning to do the usual shower
and shave.

"Well, good morning," I said to the little green frog who was sitting on
the edge of the wash basin looking up at me with his dark eyes, "are you
ready for your morning walk." I took him gently, closed my hand about
the wriggling remonstration, walked down the stairs, into the yard.

I opened my hand.

He hesitated and then jumped.

Really, things are only as they should be on the edge of the basin and in
the tall green grass.

I Water New Sown Grass

It is August and the days are hot. I water new sown grass in the cool of the morning, planted, as it was, against better judgment. Two weeks have passed and the tender green spikes push at scattered straw. The gold of straw and green of grass blur together, gauze of conflict woven by birth and burden. There's beauty in the softness of this struggle to push aside old protections no longer needed. All around this little patch of newly greening, the morning over-spray has quenched the dog-day thirst of the older ones. They straighten tall and emerald-strong in the wet remembering of April.

The Aggravation of a Hundred Mes

There is a fly in my house. He has been there a week, or at least six days. I don't quite remember. I have no swatter. He is wily and I can't get close enough to him to clap him between my hands. That would be the best way to destroy him. I could kill him and applaud his death in one motion. If I were standing when I did it, his week's performance would be hailed by a standing ovation. What a glorious way to die, not in vein but in honor of universal flyness. I know it is the same fly that came buzzing in when I was putting weather stripping around my door last Saturday (oh yes, six days) because, on occasion, he will fly close by, just to aggravate what he perceives as bunches of mes, and I can see the kidney-shaped mole on his right testicle. (If I said the mole is tiny, would it be an overstatement?) At least he won't be laying eggs and hatching larvae. Or, is a fly one of those creatures that, when you say, "go fuck yourself," it has a whole other meaning?

RIDING WITH THE MOON

Mourn Not the Crippled Deer

I looked up.
Winter had vanished.

The wind has calmed itself.
Tall pines that edge Denali's woods
move slowly with the spirit of a dying storm.
Their pallid green needles brush
hush-a-by-rock-a-by whispers to nesting birds.
The forsythia is brilliant.

Right beside the back door,
grape hyacinth and daffodils bloom full,
color begging for a human touch.
Grass is growing wild and rumpled green.
Signs the geese will soon be leaving Spanish Pond
Their harsh and trailing voices
calling egrets to return.

The egrets follow the sun.
I sit on the porch swing in the morning
and watch them, necks essed back, legs trailing,
wings spread in awesome length and grace,
disappear over the locust thicket,
into the sunrise.
At evening coffee, the egrets seem to
burst up out of the thicket
and chase the sun over me and into the west.

I never cross the road and walk into the locust grove.
When the trees have dropped their fragrance
like a summer snow
and the cool, perfumed evenings give in
to the warm breath of a full day of sun,
the locust trees leaf out along with attendant brush.
A family of five deer bed there
concealed from breezes that would carry
their deer smell to wild dogs and coyotes.

Porch swing June morning all pink and mauve
and orange ribbons flowing
from the dark edges of the sky
and disappearing with the egrets
into the vast, bright, burning ball
that is all but hidden by the trees.

In skittish hesitation the deer approach the road.
Then, in turn, each fixes me with black inquiring eyes,
hesitates again then crosses,
the last one hobbling with her twisted leg.
They vanish quickly into Denali's woods.

At evening coffee,
the egrets have chased the sun to darkness.
Four deer have returned to leafy sanctuary.
The coyotes in Denali's woods
have silenced their quarrel over death.

When the moon is full and
rises out of the locust trees on a clear night
and shadows lay sharp across the yard
and the night creatures celebrate evensong,
when this happens ...
that is all there needs to be.

I Could No Longer See the Moon

Had it been the sun,
I would have been driving to work about noon today,
but it was the moon,
at least a half moon on the waning side of full
and so pale in the dawn
behind the promises of rain—
colorless companion, spirit glance, faceless,
I felt like we,
the moon and I, were riding west together.
We were floating silent in the stillness
of the dawn,
she in the emptiness of space,
I in a stream of traffic.
We spoke to one another, in a reflective sort of way,
about the west's horizon,
both of us, as it were, on the dwindling side of life.
"Did you ever notice," she asked, "that just before
the sun and I drop below the western rim,
our colors are their richest,
our images their largest?"
As anticipation of a revelation precedes the sunrise,
"Yes," I said," yes."
"Well, don't make too much of it,"
she said.
"It is an illusion."
The highway curved to the south,
I could no longer see the moon.

Ama Jiggy

Ama Jiggy walks along the beach,
barefoot in the sand, the sunrise
waiting for her call,
long abandoned conch clutched
in her small and wrinkled hand.
She stops and turns into the east,
resists the tug about her feet
waits, then resists again.
She smiles,
the empty shell held to her ear
then again against her breast,
turns and walks along that line
where receding surf
pulls the sand from beneath
defiant feet—
pulls in vain—
pulls at Ama Jiggy.

My weathered age made by wind and salt
I listen to your ancient cries—you to mine—
there is no trace of me upon your sand
forgotten mother that I am.

Ama Jiggy walks in darkness,
she does not hide but avoids a glance
from man or woman else they be seduced
by this form of age and beauty
to cast their broken hearts into the surf.

Moving with the rhythm of the sea,
dressed in kelp from shifting currents,
she steps deliberately upon the edge of salt,
dark eyes feasting on the least of shadows
where fear may seek its refuge,
where evil waits its chance—her smile.
She touches softly the shell to ear
and then to breast and then her
lips where whispers disappear into the shell
and call her lover to appear,
to dissolve her
in his arms of memory light.

When I rose from you my name was Eden
then I lay with my creator,
yielded quickly my fertility—gave birth to man.
Man forgets yet I remain his mother.

Ama Jiggy now faded pink and mauve into the east,
her garment taken by the tide,
walks along that line where tomorrow dwells,
calls like receding memories or dreams.
Her naked beckoning resisted—unknown
urgings pulling at the feet—resisted.
The surf licks an abandoned shell that
waits for life to claim the emptiness
and smell the sweet, sweet breath of
Eden.

Going to Work on a February Day After Having Eaten Week-old Chicken Salad for Breakfast

Stuff all over the ground—
white, cold, slick afoot—
melting on the heated windshield
beneath the intermittent wipers
that keep my world clear and
somewhat safe.
Soft and mellow voices
drift from NPR
speak to me of disease
      pestilence
             the war
and global warming—
mind drifts, gouging lakes
of deep imagination,
then withdraws
like the receding ice cap
that once reached southern Minnesota
(why now the urgency?)

On the parking lot,
at work,
the pavement is slick with sleet
that melts in spots, beneath exhaust pipes.
The walk from car to office is treacherous
today.
I shall slip and fall—
then in a hundred thousand years

be chipped from ice,
the contents of my stomach
studied
by astounded scientists who look like
upright woolly mammoths
and exclaim,
"a carnivore!"

I Never Did Care For Brahms

January cold held tight
to night skies of star silver
moon yellow Mad Hatter grin
creeping over treetops
laughing at the feebleness
of dark days
and their coffin cars with
rubber wheels, glass lids
and oh yessssss
the humming of the engine
its warm refreshing breath
brings solitude
and the restfulness of
deserted driveways
through lengths of garden hose.
In the deep hours,
after telephones are silenced,
January cold drops the crystal
hoary
shroud
like countless stars
across the windshield
of this tomb
while the radio
plays
Brahms.

Receiving Line

There ain't no St. Peter
no dean of admissions
sitting at an old, oak desk
giving a freshman a load of crap
when he steps off the boat,
the one that brought him
across the River Styx.

St. Peter ain't standin' at the golden gate.
There ain't no golden gate.
That's me in a ghetto-white tux
with a big ass grin on my face
flashing a single gold tooth
at the folks diddy-boppin' by
offering handshakes and hugs.

Like I'm a bridegroom in a receiving line
no bride, no parents of, just me
looking clean and fresh and ready to party
with these old, dead relatives and close friends
all these old familiar faces walkin' by
singin' "God's Gonna Trouble da Water."
So I'll follow this Bunny Hop line to the river.

No, not the Styx, this one flows with
milk and honey and eddies gracefully
around the gold boulders of the levy,
bathing and protecting the last remaining

bluefin tuna in its deep soothing currents.
You know everybody's image of
there must be something better

like life without sushi, and house cats;
the ultimate reward for tolerating all
the trials and tribulations bestowed by
a loving God upon such a wretch as me
and you and St. Peter, the rock and foundation
upon which the Sistine Chapel was built.
Heavens! I have strayed from the straight

and narrow path of righteousness. I best focus
least Gabriel sound that godforsaken horn,
to get my attention, and call every assoul in
creation to judgment and spoil my reception.
Where was I? . . . trials and tribulations like
the Jews doing genocide, the Christian Inquisition
or the twenty-first century Islamic jihad.

Ah, forget religion and stuff; this is my party,
a time for singin' and dancin', maybe some nookie;
lots of good lookin' stuff comin' through this line.
Hi angel who's your friend?
Can't be God.
She's too short and
her breath smells like automobile exhaust.

God's Breath

Fog comes early and
lingers long at Spanish Pond.
Being in a muffled world
things are soft—
not harsh,
not well defined.
Whisper to yourself.
Pretend there is some living thing
beyond the damp, gray shroud.
Imagine unreal shapes.
Pretend that they,
for some forgotten reason,
matter.
All I want to do is drift
weightless as this mist
into the fog and sleep
upon the surface of Spanish Pond
or condense into a tear,
drop from something hard and cold
into black water of the pond,
exciting silver crested ripples
to forever kiss deserted banks,
to caress the brown and brittle reeds.

Children of Another Cat

The day came softly on cat's feet
Creeping up behind
My deep sleep
Tugging at the blanket
Pulled about my ears
Purring loudly
Rhythms of necessity that
Echo quietly through
Dark December rooms
Demanding attention like
Love-starved-loneliness.
Be still, be still
Children of my doing
Offspring of inane activities
That accomplish naught but wealth
And that of little value.

Be gone old cat
To the barn and chase
The mice around the hay bails
Or lap spilled milk.
I shall listen to the music
Of the blind and deaf
Or contemplate the art of
A crazy man.

Christmas in the Mountains

It is a strange thing, the past.
The Ozark Mountain range,
and Appalachian too,
was flat, then tall,
now just a string of
modest hills
that gives no consideration
to their strata
born of passion
welcomed to the present
by persistence and
resistance
to wind and rain.
Experience eroded,
cut the lines of character
then molded smooth.
Ozark and Appalachian
do not remember,
stand peaceful
in the beauty of the
present,
accept the future.
But I recall
and strive to be
alive in yesterday,
to seek a taller time,
put a face on passion,
and to find the perfect
Christmas tree.

Contrasts

Monochromatic grey,
February morning
thick and soft
with clouds and mist;
silent
ice building
where salt has not been cast,
no foot-crunch on my walk
up the slippery drive,
no crackle of a breaking crust
to announce my presence,
no living thing
to acknowledge my presence;
this grey and fragile figure
moving with staccato steps
beneath the black and barren locust trees.
There is only grey silence.
There is only cold silence.

Engine of the pickup warms the cab;
mellow green dash lights
whisper unneeded information;
from the speakers, Zeppelin's "Black Dog"
loud and loud and loud,
filling the grey silence of February
with screaming life.
I drive to work slowly—
on slushy roads.

Femina's Garden

Endless searching for Femina
through this lush green garden
that caresses the ceaseless,
quenching stream
like two lovers alone
in a forgotten universe.
Stream and garden forever one,
a single star,
a far-off memory in time
before parable turned to truth,
before ego slithered into
self-righteous understanding.

Plucked from my side,
I embraced Femina
then denied her.
Time and age blur
the image of her grace.
My search nears end.
Invocations silenced
by this emptiness
I tire of torment.
My searching call a
forlorn echo in my hollow chest
and Femina busy tending roses
does not hear.

At evening, garden breeze,
sweet familiar fragrance
carries with it restless
yearnings to surrender,
to sacrifice this endless search to
the god of sleep.
I dine on bread and wine
then recline on cool white sheets.
The morning golden sun warms
our naked bodies while
I kneel beside Femina
and we tend the roses.

Restoration of Bert's Cabinet

It was an occupation without intent,
something to draw the focus from dejection,
from the shame of unemployment.
It was a distraction resulting in
a ragged collection of tools,
chemicals and abrasives
scattered about an arbitrary justification
for eroded decorative whims and
laid-back, brushed-on changes,
green on blue on pink on white,
a covering for each generation.
Colors laid in chips, and floated,
suspended in goop on the cold concrete.
Time passed into revelation.
And the thing became the knowing
and the knowing drew me into it.
The shades gave in to forgetting.
The coarse oak grain clung to the white,
reluctant but then surrendering its first sin.
At the end of this was the restoration of
Bert's cabinet, a Hoosier cabinet, original
with the exception of modern hardware,
it stood beautiful in the innocence of newness,
above the chips and goop.

***

Who Bert was was a mystery,
other than she was family
and had a cabinet named for her,
an acquired name, a point of distinction,
else who would remember Bertha
or Bert's daughter Alice?
There is one but
then the vodka must be trusted
and the telling picked from
mellow long distance silences,
sifted from the dead pain
that has been heaped upon
some cold hard past.
There is a want to hear more than the quiet
plastic pressed against an ear.
There is an expectation of some great wisdom,
a fantastic revelation buried
deep in the porous conversation
and indeed there was

                    ***

"Alice was so hot-to-trot that after a date,
she had her young man on the front lawn.
Everybody in town talked about it,

how hot-to-trot Alice was.

It didn't make any difference that Bert
painted her kitchen and everything in it white
including that beautiful oak Hoosier cabinet.

Except she didn't paint the cook stove.

It got too hot."

***

Bert's Cabinet stands beautiful and pristine
the centerpiece in a country kitchen
surrounded by copper-bottomed pots and
cast-iron skillets to compliment her age.
An abused servant of four generations
of an exquisitely dysfunctional family,
now an icon of redemption for
an alcoholic, a town hussy and
whatever it is I am.

Bittersweet

Swirl honey in the tea of bitter herbs.
Stir with a silver spoon and lazy motion,
hot spoon clinks on fine bone china,
milky white and lipped with gold,
the hollow chime makes fragile ripples
dance above the settling leaves.
Lean to the cup and let the fragrance
of the heat blend sweet and bitter
in olfactory praise of earth and sun fire.
Dare to read the sleeping fragments
spread across reflections of inquiring eyes.
Dare to read their restless dreams
and learn to mix their joy and sorrow
then raise the golden rim up to your lips
and sip the bittersweet refreshment.
Sip again and end your thirst.

Julie @ poet.com

I do not know you
but for a brief hello,
a casual introduction, a passing nod,
touching hands in simple etiquette.
If something passed between us
my hand does not remember
nor do my ears recall your voice
when searching playful melodies
that fill the background silences
in past halls of darkness.

I do not know you,
yet struggle not to fall in love.
We walk in silent conversation
through the fertile fields and unmapped valleys,
across the golden, shifting, e-lectronic dunes.
Image without form, fleeting shadows
avoid the grasp of meditating eyes,
imagination lost between heart and mind,
a ghost of everything held dear,
a ghost of every poem
my soul could ever write.

I do not know you but as artist.
It is your lot to bear your being full to others,
to share your beauty, share your pain.
Then you bless me, asking for my spirit
to take a deeper drink than most would dare

from the chalice of your life.
The dark red words of harvest revelations
flood my senses till shadows are the only
focus of my love and drift between the art and artist.

I know the shadows well but only reason at the light.
So I will end this struggle now,
give myself in full surrender
to love the flower of your words.
To hold creator captive in my heart
would doubtless wilt the blossoms of creation.

Reception

Dark eyes, a face of somber joy
Tell your story without revealing details.
Smooth brown shoulders and slender arms
Set the richness of ivory cloth and pearls
That spills to polished planks without a splash.

Beauty goes beyond the music
The force of motion, gliding feet.
I know who you are. You told me.
But yesterday dances with its own partner.
Hold your lover close. Recall the future.

Background voices share secret conversations
Punctuated by delighted laughter. They celebrate,
Looking for reflections of their hopes—and prayers.
You are their flawless mirror giving clarity
Asking nothing in return. You have no need.

The music stops then a voice begins new melody.
You are aware of me, a smile. I come to you,
Hold you in my arms. "Who gives this woman?"
Your head rests on my shoulder. "Her mother and I."
I know the joy of dancing with daughters.

Change

Sometimes you know it's coming.
Sometimes you walk out the door
and it's just hanging there,
suspended from nothing,
invisible beneath the ribbons of sunrise,
silent beneath the creature noises of small things.
But, you know it's there
and you turn,
and you go back into the house,
and you don't know why.
Some forgotten item greets you from the kitchen table—
your go-cup, a bill to be mailed,
a vase of cut flowers for a sick friend, a lover.

Still, it's there,
something watching over your shoulder
as you dead bolt away
the hidden treasures of your labors,
the years of resonating echoes, voices of dear companions,
the muttered meditations born of unexpected loneliness,
the flickering images of candlelight dinners.

Sometimes you know it's coming,
rustling through the grass or
gliding like the egret—silent, with grace.

Sometimes you know it's coming.
You want to name it and
cannot.

Pond Master

Cold touches my face.
It is a source of conversation
As I walk around the pond.
The cold is welcomed.
It is welcomed as any season
Coloring thoughts with
Unfamiliar shades of reason.

Retracing footsteps each tomorrow,
Cold and then the wind
Becomes less friendly.
I turn my back on them,
Avoid their argument.
I feign to love the elements
But seek their comfort not their torment.

The geese trace the Mississippi
Every autumn, escape the thunder
Of the hunter's guns,
Break from the larger flock,
Then boisterous but on graceful wing
Come claim this pond as home
And stay to welcome back the spring.

The flock is my companion now,
Just aware of me.
Softly mutter conversations
Within their congregation.

Millennia of ancestral voices
Churning water, holding back the ice.
For them there are no other choices.

Coyote and wild dog
Howling to their spirit god
Icy moon-glint on the snowy pond
Geese preserve a ring of darkness
Speak restlessly and echo warning.
There is no salvation's plan.
One will die before the morning.

The pond is all that welcomes me.
So, at sunset, I sit and watch
Huddled by a friendly fire.
While dog and coyote both complain,
The restless geese sing acclamation
To the Fire and Me. I starve the dogs.
I Am the birds' salvation.

Down The Mississippi

Revelation (I've had only one)
is the sudden appearance of
a truth you have known
even before your birth.
It is a chromosome
woven into the DNA of
some endless oversoul.

Sitting on the Missouri River levee,
just above the Mississippi,
I plucked my righteous thought
from a small piece of drift wood
white and bouncing
like a marshmallow
in an endless stream of
spiced chai tea.

I inhaled the pungent fragrance
of that sweet inspiration
just as a spank-assed babe
sucks in life.
The first exhale of this new life—
"You have a God-given
right to sin…."
I will follow this murky current to
New Orleans.

The Highway

Joshua, long deserted son,
reached into his magic
chest of toys, brought forth
forgiveness and nursed me
through the pain of loss—
companion to a widower—
now companion in my travels.

We packed some clothes
then left for New Orleans—
a rented Chevy,
Josh behind the wheel.
All ownership abandoned—
there were no ties to home
except the highway never ends.

In the boot heel of Missouri
just south of Sikeston,
the highway rose (just a bit)
then it dipped back down.
This last Missouri hill gave way
to long-forgotten swamps.
Faded cypress groves then
cotton fields gave in to
flooded squares of rice.
Cottonmouths remain
and the highway does not stop.

Beneath our conversation,
we buried well the boredom
of greedy devastation.
I told stories from my past.
Josh spoke of plans and dreams.
Somewhere along our path
from past to future
Missouri disappeared.
So we counted
dead and dying armadillos
along the wooded
Mississippi highway.

A Different Now

Josh and I had no desire
to step into the past.
History, as the future,
held no purpose.
So, the Saint James was fine—
a place to shower,
a place to rest.

The Saint James
had a young and fresh façade.
Her style reflected
old and brittle bones.
Architects of illusion
like plastic surgeon pimps
had worked their will on her.
Her strength was there
but her colors hard,
her brass—too shiny.

Josh carried an old Pentax
I had given him
loaded with black and white.
He captured timeless,
monochromatic,
two-dimensional
realities
that were the worlds
of strangers' faces.

Historic buildings—
just backgrounds
by incidental artisans.
Why New Orleans?
Why travel?
"Saint Louis is different ...
It has a different ... now."

The son will teach the father
if the father listens.
I understood
my wispy, troubled
nebula of memory.
Praying for a breeze
I stepped from the Saint James' lobby
onto Magazine Street,
into the shimmering stillness of
New Orleans.

Faceless Men

A coffee house, smoked-glass front—
my table looked upon the street.
A sturdy chair of comfort—
shiny onyx tabletop.
Free of summer heat,
I sipped chicory and watched
the sacred sentry
through a glass darkly.

He was not a homeless man.
The doorway was his home—
a big door, a loading dock door
not like the entryways
of the Bourbon Street clubs
where small confessionals
protected priestly come-on girls
while they listened to
the lines of faceless men.

He was always home,
that ragged man with possessions
stuffed into a plastic milk crate.

He was always there
when I left the Saint James Hotel,
walked north to The Quarter.
I only glimpsed him.
I dared not stare but

accumulated knowledge through
cowardly, sideways glances.

He was always there,
a motionless, weathered
piece of ebony like a
carved and chiseled totem
placed as a warning
by forgotten tribes.

I longed to cross the street
to stare into his eyes
to find what placed him there.
I was afraid his soul
would be as empty
as his warehouse.
I was afraid
I might know him.

Canal Street

By choice or
unwritten law,
tattered beggars,
the unwashed
the unwanted,
do not cross
Canal Street.
They place their
static lives
in the shade of
abandoned buildings
and stoically watch
the creeping renovation.

Canal Street—
boulevard ribbed with
steel bones, electric energy—
old time trolleys
skirting would be pilgrims along
the edge of a holy city—
where Magazine Street
passes through the
eye of the needle
and becomes Decatur
and Decatur penetrates
into the heart of
the French Quarter.
At sundown

families vanish from
this sacred ground.
The god we worship here
recoils from their innocence
so the children, like the
ragged men, wait
outside the temple walls
while the religious right—
ecstatic and dogmatic,
pray with hardened nipples,
beneath the wrought-iron altars,
for plastic beads of
salvation.

Come-on Girl

Bourbon Street nightclubs
blend their music
along garbage-lined curbs.
Passing from the harshness
and anger of rock music
into the painful throat of blues
and the cry of purgative jazz.
I deny the odor of lunchtime,
forgotten gumbo
baked by late afternoon heat,
pause by an open doorway
to drift with
the soul of a jazzman.
We ride on a l—o—n—g E flat
into a dark night sky
hidden by neon glare.

A voice sings beneath
the throaty-brass reed.
It is not my song
but pulls me back
into the glare of
where I am.

I stare into the empty eyes
of a come-on girl.
Her body beckons well
sitting in the doorway,

face veiled with makeup.
She tugs the beads around my neck
to pull me in
as did her hollow melody.
Her whisper smells of roses.

"Pay the price to enter
the smoke-soft room.
Sip some dark red wine."
I finger my beaded collar
and share the wa wa trumpet
with the fading vision of the
come-on girl.

Shattered remnants of my sin
lie by the neon curb.
This feast demands
a contrite and honest heart.
Hail Eros full of life,
be with us now
in the name of
The Jazzman
The Come-on girl
And Me

Fun

An aluminum, cowboy mime,
tableau of fun, will move
for a dollar bill … or
let you take a picture.

Preservation Hall, where ancient souls
with young hearts play old music
in musty, crowded darkness,
sells Dixie Jazz to animated tourists.

A scam artist will tell her story
to a background of violin and clarinet.
It is fun to let yourself get used by words
and part, foolishly, with a five or ten.

The canopied and entertaining walk
past the French-market shops that sell
Cajun spice, red beans and rice also
lure you to the voodoo dolls … "how's your ex?"

You will find smiling workers heaping plates
with grits and sausages and scrambled eggs
for business folks and travelers
if you make the early bird at Mother's.

Josh and I left Mother's and New Orleans.
The causeway crossed swampy land.
For many miles our tires sang a dirge
over specks of drowning northern plains.

We headed for Missouri—back the way we came.
Conversations of the fun times faded
into shiny plastic CD jazz and blues.
I laid my head back, closed my eyes.

"Where will we go next year?" Josh asked.
The question cut an almost sleep. I did not hear
but felt the answer stumble past my lips, "Calcutta."
"Cool ... but I can't buy that much film."

I kissed their cheeks goodbye, the children, the
come-on girls, and ragged men then awoke to
a mean and awful sky. It was our welcome home—
the fury of Good Friday.

Down The Mississippi
(again)

Sitting on the Missouri River levee
just above the Mississippi,
I focus softly on the shore beyond—
blurring woods that
gently wrap the life within ...
as the fun of New Orleans
obscures what tourists
do not want to see.
The deer needs her woods.
I need my distractions
but the laughter fades
and my tears fall like crystals
to this clear, bright stream.
I wonder at the driftwood
white and bouncing
like a blossom,
of ten thousand petals,
on the Great Tai Chi.